After the Tumbles and Tangles

A Guide to Good Thoughts

Angie Salamah

BALBOA.
PRESS

A DIVISION OF HAY HOUSE

Balboa Press books may be ordered through booksellers or by contacting:

Balboa Press
A Division of Hay House
1663 Liberty Drive
Bloomington, IN 47403
www.balboapress.com.au
1 (877) 407-4847

Because of the dynamic nature of the Internet, any web addresses or
links contained in this book may have changed since publication and
may no longer be valid. The views expressed in this work are solely those
of the author and do not necessarily reflect the views of the publisher,
and the publisher hereby disclaims any responsibility for them.

The author of this book does not dispense medical advice or prescribe
the use of any technique as a form of treatment for physical, emotional,
or medical problems without the advice of a physician, either directly
or indirectly. The intent of the author is only to offer information
of a general nature to help you in your quest for emotional and
spiritual well-being. In the event you use any of the information in
this book for yourself, which is your constitutional right, the author
and the publisher assume no responsibility for your actions.

Any people depicted in stock imagery provided by Thinkstock are
models, and such images are being used for illustrative purposes only.
Certain stock imagery © Thinkstock.

Print information available on the last page.

ISBN: 978-1-5043-0411-5 (sc)
ISBN: 978-1-5043-0412-2 (e)

Balboa Press rev. date: 09/05/2016

For my two beautiful girls who bring sunshine to my soul.
I love you endlessly.
You are my greatest treasures.
May you always feel loved, belonged and understood. Never stop believing and dreaming.

To my Husband, without you my treasures would never have been possible, may we soar to new heights.

To my tumbles and tangles, Thank you, without you I never would have found me.
And this book would not have been possible.

My Family who always offer enlightenment,

To my Mum, I am your greatest admirer.

For those who feel alone, I hope my words bring you some warmth.

God who carries me through it all.

Introduction

Games of the heart; thoughts from the mind. The endless cycle of one's own inquiry about life. The few words that I began writing became a thousand pages. Words that helped me through a day; others saw me through what seemed like a never-ending night.

These pages are a part of my heart and soul. In these words are moments of sentiment. Moments when I have questioned life and its contradictions. Moments I thought this world was cold, unforgiving, and completely unjust.

Equal to the pain, there have been times of abundant joy and thankfulness for being here. I am grateful for all my memories and for the chances I have had to experience many cocktails of emotions.

I truly believe the outcome of something bad will result in something greater than you can imagine. This may be hard to believe in the circumstance of pain or loss. However, persist in what you believe, even if it is not clearly visible at the time. Your emotional instability will come to rest.

Our emotional world will never cease. Something tells me to prevail because things will make sense to all of us one day. In the meantime, we must be grateful for what we have, be kind, and to keep being positive in your outlook. I am still learning to digest life. Perhaps that is what it is all about!

$\mathscr{F}$eed your body with healthy food.
Feed your mind with good thoughts and expectations.
Feed your soul with love and kindness.
Feed today with happiness,
and visualize all the beautiful
experiences your heart desires for
a wonderful tomorrow.

$\mathscr{L}$earn to live abundantly.
In abundance of all that is good:
Abundant love,
Abundant joy,
Abundant laughter.
Let your heart be full, your soul content,
and your smile a mile long.
Refuse negativity;
Fight back with kindness.

$\mathscr{Y}$our exceptional self is waiting
For you to change your mind to
a positive way of being.
Change your mind, and see how your life changes!

$\mathcal{T}$he universe doesn't care if you make mistakes.
Neither should you.
Mistakes are necessary for you to learn and grow.

$\mathscr{Y}$ou can have what your heart desires;
First, your mind must desire what you seek.

*T*o change the big stuff in your life, you must begin
with the small stuff.
Huge accomplishments begin with
changing how you perceive things.
Prescribe yourself some happiness, and see
how your world begins to improve.

*A*lways remember
The light shines brightest in your darkest hours.

$\mathcal{T}$he best thing about hitting rock bottom is that the only way to go is up.

$\mathcal{T}$hose who think they know it all know nothing.

$\mathcal{Y}$our dreams won't fly unless you give them wings.

$\mathscr{I}$f you don't love yourself, honour yourself,
and respect yourself,
Why would you expect someone else to?

Remember, if respect doesn't live there,
Love doesn't either.

$\mathcal{H}$appiness grows; plant seeds of love and smiles daily.

$\mathcal{Y}$our thoughts are a magnetic energy force.
Realize the power of your thoughts, and
Release good things with good intentions and beliefs.
Manifest your own beautiful world.

$\mathscr{Y}$ou have subconsciously attracted every person and
situation into your life.
Consciously, it's time to be aware of
your thoughts and belief systems.
That is what will ultimately define you.

*I*t is in your darkest hour when you will see your
brightest light.

*T*he things you silently tell yourself have the most
impact in your life.
Be mindful of what you feed your soul.
Be kind with your words to others.
Be soft with your thoughts of yourself.
Be infrequent with your self-criticism.
Be optimistic of your future.
Be forgiving of your faults.
Be good to your body; it is the house of your spirit.
Be aware of your weaknesses.
Be more proactive of your strengths.
Be fair in your opinions of others;
You never know what struggles
their heart is harbouring.
Be true to yourself; lying to yourself is like closing your eyes
When you're in front of the mirror.
Lies will not serve you well in the long run.
Be happy in the moment if you can; each
day that passes you cannot get back.
Be compassionate; it is the essence of humanity.
Be your best self always; life is too
short for anything less.
Be grateful for the beautiful things in your life.
If you pay attention, you will see
Your time here is the greatest gift.

$\mathcal{D}$o not force situations.
Letting go allows for things to work out
in their due time.
God opens millions of buds every day
without forcing the flower.

*I*n order to discover new oceans, you need to lose
sight of the shore.
Do not fear the unknown.
Embrace it, and allow for it to take
you to wonderful places.

$\mathscr{B}$e free within the realms of your mind.
Allow your thoughts to soar like an eagle,
And transform the negative into positive.
With clarity, be firm in the belief
that all is as it should be.

$\mathscr{A}$midst a barricade of darkness,
A fog of loneliness,
A thought will arise within the depth of
yourself that will somehow set you free.

$\mathcal{B}$y clinging to past thoughts, we become
unavailable to the present.
Do not collect, accumulate, or
cling to negative thoughts.
Let it go and watch.
It will recede, making room for the good.

$\mathscr{T}$he only limitations are those we set upon ourselves.
When we conquer negativity, we conquer failure.
Thoughts crystallize.

$\mathcal{A}$ soul that aspires for contentment will
never fail to rise.
In the quiet of your mind is where you
will find what enriches you.
Crave for love with all its richness.

$\mathcal{A}$llow love to rejuvenate your soul.
Allow tenderness to chase away the shadows of doubt.
Allow yourself to live in the moment, uninterrupted.
Allow yourself the opportunity to
create a life of excellence.

$\mathcal{W}$e are designed intricately, and
God has handcrafted us delicately.
Learn to handle yourself with care.

$\mathcal{W}$ith every conscious and unconscious thought you are creating your world.

$\mathcal{G}$etting to know yourself is refreshing and
strengthening.

$\mathscr{A}$llow the outskirts of your mind to be traced
with some kind of wonderful.
Even in the uncertainty of what it may be,
Await it in faith.

$\mathcal{Y}$ou must surrender to the belief
That you will receive all you deserve.

$\mathcal{L}$ove is the only thing
That we cannot buy, manufacture, control, or even
explain at times.
It is something that is seated deeply within us all.
Open the door within yourself,
And set it free.

$\mathcal{W}$hen you are walking through a web of fears,
Let the light within yourself walk you through.

$\mathcal{F}$eel satisfied in knowing
That sometimes—even when you have
done all you can,
And things didn't turn out the way you'd have liked—
There may something bigger and better
Waiting for you to arrive.

$\mathcal{L}$ove should be like a steady light burning.
A lantern of joy
Where desires and dreams burn for eternity.

$\mathscr{Y}$ou have within you the invisible strength
To see you through your struggles.
It is there.

$\mathcal{W}$hen you learn to see with your soul,
You can see everything with your eyes shut.

$\mathcal{W}$e often make or break our worlds
By our manners of thinking.
Leave good imprints in your mind.

$\mathscr{B}$e happy.
Dance to the beat of your soul.

*I*n the valley of heart
Lies hidden a wonderful waterfall.

*H*ope is the tiny seed
From which a spectacular tomorrow can grow.

$\mathcal{Y}$ou can make your sky whatever colour you like.
Pick a colour!

*M*ay our ships again meet
in the same harbour and sail to a journey beyond.

There are a million thoughts, kisses, and dreams
I want only with you.

I experience a feeling of absolute stillness—
a surging rush of enlightenment.
Reflecting on all the yesterdays does me
no justice for where I am today.
All is new and unfamiliar; a new day has
formed with a new vision and outlook.
It proves how living in the present really matters
And that even today will become an hour of the past.
Live each day to its fullest.
Live each day with love in your heart and
desire in your soul.
Moments have become years, and a
minute becomes a lifetime.

You know you are my heart's desire.
Regardless of all, you are now a memory
vivid in my heart.
The good remains as a dream that
I play back in my mind.
When I daydream,
I attempt to create a harmonious, placid world in
which to rest my heart.
The constant battle is to forget;
Trying to suppress my thoughts does me no justice.
Instead, I allow the release to move past this feeling
That is like a volcanic eruption.

$\mathcal{I}$ take each day at a time,
And pray for the best.
As hard as the days get and as torturous as my
nights are,
I strive for the hope that one day soon
my prayers will be answered,
And I will find my peace, my place.
Meanwhile, I talk to my angels
And tell myself that they are holding me safe.

*T*ears are useless
When passion has moved you far
from what you know.
How do you fill the void?
How do the nights end?
What gives you comfort and warmth?
What choices have brought you difficulty, great
difficulty?

Simplicity appears to be more appealing.
They say inside is where the answers are;
Inside you is a roller coaster,
A place where you enter and get
lost in a maze of yourself.
This puzzle of emotions will soon subside.
You will find yourself in the better place you seek.
Feeling the pain
Is part of the process of renewal and growth.
Persevere;
You will get there soon.

*I*f love were a definition,
Love is the light in a dark room.
Love is the uplifting feeling that kicks
you along when you are down.
Love is the invisible strength
That gives you courage when all seems to be failing.
Love is what can fill the empty void of loneliness.
Love is lying in your arms and feeling
that the world is at your feet.
Love is what is invisible to the eye
but felt with the heart.
Love is the fluttering of butterflies in your belly.
Love knows in a moment what you have
been looking to find for a lifetime.
Love is felt in you like *schweppervescence,*
That rush to the top of a bottle in a fizzy drink.

You crept through the doors of my heart,
The ones I forgot I left open.
You touched parts of my spirit that
I didn't know existed.
You calmed all the rage.
You woke my sleeping soul that had
lost its way for little while.
You hijacked my soul,
And now I am swimming in a sea of love
and drowning in its depth.

$\mathcal{D}$on't be too hard on yourself for your mistakes; your
life is the stage for which you didn't get to rehearse.
Your performance is about what you
gain from your mistakes.

$\mathscr{B}$eautiful is the spirit of a broken person, smiling at you like he or she has it all.

*I*t is what you cannot see that you need to believe
in the most.

$\mathscr{A}$ poor person has something the wealthiest person can't buy—a rich heart.

$\mathscr{M}$ake sure your actions of today are something
you can be proud of tomorrow.

$\mathscr{A}$ weak person sees difficulties.
A strong person sees opportunities.

*T*o come first makes you a winner; to come last but still feel like a winner makes you a champion.

$\mathscr{T}$o appreciate good, we must see the bad.

A rich person who can be bought is no better than a poor person who can be sold.
Your integrity is something you should never trade.

*W*hen you're pushed, you must learn how to fly.

$\mathcal{W}$hat you seek you should find within yourself
first.

$\mathcal{O}$pen the doors of your mind without hesitation,
The doors of heart without reservation,
And surrender yourself to the
knowledge that you find there.

$\mathcal{O}$ne smile can soften a thousand burdens.

*F*ear is good; it moves beyond your comfort zone.
Fear takes you to places you never
would reach without it.

$\mathcal{T}$he best life you will get is the best life you can imagine for yourself. Dream big.

$\mathcal{Y}$ou have now; you have this minute to do
with it what you will.
Why then worry about the yesterday that you cannot
change or the tomorrow that is not yet here?
Today will become a moment of the
past, and the moment is too precious to
waste on the pain of yesterday.
You never know how one moment can transform
your life from one to minute to the next.
And you don't know what awaits tomorrow.
Enjoy the now; this is what you have.

$\mathcal{D}$o the opposite of what you hate.

$\mathcal{Y}$ou can never lose what was never yours.

$\mathcal{B}$e kind to others and kindest to yourself.

$\mathcal{D}$on't suppress your feelings; doing so will make your spirit sick.

*W*hen you are ready, take away your mask.
Gently take by the hand the inner child who has been
hiding in corners of your soul. Give that
part of yourself love and sunshine.

*I*f all were forgotten, what would you remember?

$\mathcal{S}$uccess does not exist without failure.

There is day; there is night.
There is death; there is birth.
There is rain; there is sunshine.
There is hot; there is cold.
There is bad; there is good.
There is a cycle, a natural rhythm to existence.
Rest assured that if you are now in pain,
There will be joy.

They say no one changes who they are. Maybe not. You can always, though, improve who you are.

$\mathscr{Y}$ou are given a blank, pure, clean canvas that represents your life journey.
You are given all the tools required to commence and take the path you have envisioned in your mind.
However, along the way, you will change your colours on that canvas countless times. You will make corrections and amendments. You will look at that canvas with tireless eyes and think it is complete. But you are unsatisfied with what you think is the final image. So you start all over again with a new vision or direction, and the process repeats itself.
In the end, whatever the masterpiece—your life—ends up looking like, always know it is in the imperfections that your best self is seen.

$\mathcal{W}$hen your heart has hurt so much that it has unhinged your soul, know your remedy will be found in the vaults of your mind.

$\mathcal{L}$et the passion within you run free. Suppressing your passion is like taking a beautiful, wild lion from its element and taming it to perform in a circus.

$\mathcal{D}$on't focus on the pain of yesterday.
The seat on which you once sat is not required
on the mountain on which you now stand.

*I*t's not what you say.
We can all talk.
It's what you do that screams volumes.

$\mathcal{Y}$our heart will cry a thousand rivers
Until it discovers the ocean.

*E*xcitement is like something borrowed;
it is short-lived.
Contentment is like a tree, deep-
rooted and always there.

$\mathcal{W}$hen you lose your way, stuff, make mistakes,
stumble, and fall,
Remember to move forward. You must let
go of the pain, but keep the lesson.

*I*t takes imagination to dream.
It takes courage and determination to act on it.
To bring your dreams to life,
You must move on them.
Take action.

$\mathcal{I}$t is the things you cannot see that you need to believe in the most.

$\mathscr{P}$eople who put others down are the ones who
don't know how to pull themselves up.

$\mathcal{M}$ake sure today's actions are things you can be proud of tomorrow.

$\mathcal{I}$n times of hardship,
A weak person sees difficulties.
A strong person sees opportunities.

A rich person who can be bought
Is no better than a poor person who can be sold.
Integrity is something you never trade.

$\mathcal{T}$hings are not always what they seem.
Don't assume someone is genuine by his or her attire.
It is often the rich person who has holes
in the soles of his or her shoes.

$\mathcal{W}$hen you are pushed, learn how to fly.

$\mathcal{S}$ometimes you need to fall to remind yourself
That which is beneath your feet is
what keeps you grounded.

*P*ain is the instrument that allows you to make up your own song.

*O*pen the doors of your mind without hesitation,
The doors of your heart without restriction;
Surrender yourself to the knowledge you find there.

$\mathcal{F}$ear is good; it moves beyond your comfort.
It takes you places you never would
have reached without it.

Admire strength when it is shown tenderly.

*W*hen you cry, think of it as sadness running away.

*T*ruth is the bright light in a dark room.
You can never hide truth.
If you try, you only make shadows.

$\mathcal{U}$ntil you can truly love yourself, you are not
capable of truly loving someone else.
How can teach someone to swim if you
have never been in the water?

*R*espect must be attained first within yourself.
The most important relationship in your
life is the one you have with yourself.
You must acquire love, respect, and kindness for
yourself in order to reciprocate it to others.

$\mathcal{I}$f we are faced with something unpleasant or
negative we cannot change or control,
We can make the choice to walk away from it and
not allow it to transfer onto our beautiful paths.

*T*he answer you seek is not always out there.
Learn to listen to your instinct.
Be aware of your self.
Your best answers are the ones
you find from the inside.
And the best thing about opening the door
from inside is that you never need the key.

$\mathcal{M}$ay your heart be captured by a million
breathless moments.
May a moment of happiness last you a lifetime.

$\mathcal{Y}$our love has entered my soul like
a bird flies to its nest

*W*hen you let go of your fear, you will again start
to feel alive.
You will be, with a knowing and strength
that only comes from a sense of heartache.
When you overcome it, you know
emotions were conquered.
The wisdom you gain will be to your benefit.

There are people we connect with throughout our life that even when they are far or have left this world, we still feel them everywhere.

$\mathcal{Y}$ou can never fill today's dreams with
yesterday's emptiness.

$\mathcal{W}$e humans—with all our intelligence, technology, science, and resources—still cannot define or control the force of what love can do to us.

$\mathcal{I}$f you open the door from the inside,
you do not require a key.

$\mathcal{Y}$our life is like a gift. Unwrap it to see that there is so much to celebrate.

$\mathcal{T}$here is a protective force surrounding us.
Even at times when we cannot see it,
We can feel it in our tears.
We can feel it in our laughter.
Now you are not alone.
Something very great is watching over you.

$\mathcal{E}$ven when life is presenting unpredictability
and uncertainty,
Do not let anything break your spirit.
Hold your angels close, and refuse
anything less than exceptional.

Sometimes when there are no answers in mind, it
is because the reason lies very deep in the heart.

$\mathcal{I}$n the midst of finding your way, you will
experience feelings of disorientation and confusion.
Do not fear as this is the path of transformation.
You are shedding the old to process the new.

*I*f you want it enough, there is always a way.

*M*ore often than not, your children are
reflections of you.
Make sure the mirror they are looking
at each day is the best it can be.

Don't insist on knocking on someone's heart's
door if you already know nobody lives there.

You can knock on the door of success
and wait for it to be opened.
Or you can reach for the handle, and open it yourself.

Instead of putting all your energy
into being miserable,
Put all your energy into making yourself happy.

*W*hen you were younger, what did you need most? Be that person for your children today.

*T*he most attractive thing about you will not be how you look. It will be how you think. Nothing is more stunning than a positive and beautiful thought.

Printed in the United States
By Bookmasters